DATE DUE

MOTHS and
BUTTERFLIES

MOTHS and BUTTERFLIES

DAVE BEATY

THE CHILD'S WORLD

CONTENTS

The life cycle of moths and butterflies is truly spectacular. It all begins when a tiny egg hatches and a newborn caterpillar, or *larva*, struggles free. The caterpillar begins eating immediately. Its first meal is its own eggshell.

Caterpillars stop eating only to rest or to find more food. In fact, they eat until they grow right out of their skins! This process, called *molting*, is common among all insects. After molting, the new skin soon hardens to provide protection.

A caterpillar molts three or four times before it is full grown. Then, it uses its fine silk to spin a cocoon. Inside its

cocoon, the caterpillar changes into an adult moth or butterfly.

Moths and butterflies play a crucial role in nature. When the insects feed on flower nectar, pollen from male flowers sticks to their bodies. Later, when they feed on a female plant, the pollen falls into the flower and fertilizes the egg inside. The result is a seed, which falls to the ground and grows into a flower.

There are over 150,000 species of moths and butterflies, each as unique as your thumbprint. Their survival instincts are pretty unique, too. The following are some of the many fascinating kinds of moths and butterflies.

EMPEROR MOTHS

Basking in sunshine is the emperor moth's favorite pastime. An emperor moth larva has stingers down its spine and stings anything that touches it. When building its cocoon, the caterpillar leaves a small opening on one end. It lines the opening with thorns, making it impossible for enemies to get inside. Pretty clever trick, isn't it? Emperor moths are tricky as adults, too. They have large eye spots on their wings. When a bird or rodent thinks it has a meal, the moth flashes its fake eyes. Then the butterfly makes a quick escape from the baffled enemy!

8

LUNA MOTHS

Luna moths may not be baffling, but they certainly are unforgettable. Long, flowing wings lend these insects a striking appearance. Luna moths are favorites of photographers, scientists, and nature buffs in general. Some people keep luna moths as pets. Although natives of the United States and Mexico, luna moths have been found in many parts of the world. Like emperors, luna moths also have eye spots on their wings. The luna's spots resemble small moons more than eyes. Its name, "Luna," is the Latin word for moon.

ATLAS MOTHS

Atlas moths are probably the world's biggest moths. They are sometimes mistaken for small birds flying through the forests and jungles of the Far East. The moth shown here lives in Indonesia. As you can imagine, an atlas moth caterpillar is huge—some grow to be eleven inches long! The caterpillar's cocoon looks like a large piece of fruit hanging from a tree branch. Of course, the silk used to make the cocoon must be very strong. Native people collect the cocoons and make clothing and linens from the durable silk.

SILKWORM MOTHS

Although silk from the atlas moth is highly treasured, the finest silk comes from the silkworm moth, sometimes referred to as the silk moth. No wild populations of these moths exist. Instead, they are commercially bred throughout China, the Far East, and Europe for the silk they produce. Like atlas moths, giant silkworm moths build large cocoons. Workers collect the cocoons and process them into the world's finest silk. The business of breeding silkworm moths is quite profitable because silk garments are so expensive.

14

PUSS MOTHS

The puss moth has unique ways of protecting itself. The caterpillar has fur much like a cat's, but its method of defense is more like a Ninja warrior's! When threatened by an enemy, the caterpillar raises its tail over its head and expels a red, threadlike substance. The moth twirls this over its head like a lasso. If the predator doesn't back off, the caterpillar spits acid from the top of its head. These unusual displays usually convince the attacker to look for easier prey, rather than dealing with something so peculiar.

SWALLOWTAIL BUTTERFLIES

Swallowtail butterflies have long, pointed wings that resemble the tail feathers of a bird called a swallow. Over 500 different kinds of swallowtails exist, all very large and colorful. A variety of flies and bees often seek out big caterpillars like the swallowtails' to lay their eggs on. The newborn insects then burrow into the caterpillars and eat them from the inside out. However, bees and flies don't often lay their eggs on swallowtail caterpillars. These insects are the skunks of the butterfly world. To protect themselves, they emit a horrible odor.

SULFUR BUTTERFLIES

There are over 300 kinds of sulfur butterflies. The one in this photograph is a giant sulfur, also called a cloudless sulfur. Living mainly in Mexico and the Caribbean, giant sulfurs migrate north to the United States for the winter. All sulfur butterflies have large scales covering their wings. The scales make the insects' wings very strong and durable. Though most sulfur butterflies are shaped exactly the same, they do vary in color and size. Mature giant sulfur butterflies are quite large—probably a little bigger than your hand!

AMERICAN COPPER BUTTERFLIES

American coppers are small butterflies living mainly in the northeastern United States. They prefer open, grassy areas where a plant called sheep sorrel grows. Sheep sorrel is the caterpillar's favorite food. As mature butterflies, American coppers are quite aggressive insects. They attack larger butterflies and even small birds to protect their turf. The intruder usually looks for a more peaceful place to relax. Sadly, though, American coppers are gradually disappearing. Human growth has destroyed much of the butterflies' natural habitat.

COMMON BLUE BUTTERFLIES

Common blue butterflies live throughout North America. Their caterpillars produce a fluid called *honeydew*. Ants often swarm around the larvae and sip the sweet fluid. Sometimes the caterpillars and ants work together. A butterfly larva will live inside an anthill, feeding on small ants and eggs and using the den as a cocoon. Meanwhile, the ants have an endless supply of honeydew. Once mature, the butterfly pushes its way out of the anthill. The struggle to get free makes the butterfly's wings strong enough to fly.

MONARCH BUTTERFLIES

Monarch butterflies are probably the best known of all butterflies. They are native to North America, but are found all over the world. Monarch caterpillars feed on milkweed plants. Milkweed contains a substance that is poisonous to most animals but does not affect monarch caterpillars. Any bird or rodent that eats a poison-filled monarch becomes very ill. Birds and rodents have learned to leave these colorful creatures alone. As a result, monarch caterpillars and butterflies live happily, without any predators.

VICEROY BUTTERFLIES

You aren't alone if you think this butterfly looks like the monarch on the previous page. Most birds think so, too. When the butterflies are in flight, it's nearly impossible to tell the two species apart. The viceroy's resemblance to the monarch is its main defense. Since birds know to avoid the awful-tasting monarch, they also avoid the viceroy. To keep birds confused, viceroys migrate alongside monarchs. This type of defense is called *mimicry.* Several other butterfly species also use mimicry to fool their enemies.

RED ADMIRAL BUTTERFLIES

Like monarchs, viceroys, and several other butterflies, red admirals migrate. They spend summers in northern regions throughout the world and fly south for the winter. The female butterflies lay their eggs where stinging nettle plants are abundant. The caterpillars wrap themselves in the plants' leaves and eat them. Three or four leaves wrapped together with silk make a cozy cocoon. The caterpillars try to leave the thorny leaves exposed for protection. How about a big juicy caterpillar wrapped in thorns for lunch? Thanks, but I'll stick with PB&J!

PHOTO RESEARCH

Charles Rotter/Archipelago Productions

PHOTO CREDITS

Robert & Linda Mitchell:

front cover, 4, 9, 11, 13, 15

COMSTOCK/Rose Gantner: 2

COMSTOCK/Michael Thompson: 6-7

COMSTOCK/Sharon Chester: 11

COMSTOCK/George Lepp: 19, 21, 25

COMSTOCK/Townsend Dickinson: 23, 27

J. H. Robinson: 17

E. R. Degginger: 29

Library of Congress Cataloging-in-Publication Data
Beaty, Dave, 1965-
Moths and butterflies / by Dave Beaty.
p. cm.
Summary: Describes the physical characteristics, life
cycles, and habits of a variety of moths and butterflies.
ISBN 1-56766-001-0
1. Moths--Juvenile literature.
2. Butterflies--Juvenile literature.
[1. Moths.   2. Butterflies.]   I. Title
QL544.2.B43   1993   92-29741
595.78--dc20   CIP
                                                     AC

Distributed to schools and libraries in the United States by
ENCYCLOPAEDIA BRITANNICA EDUCATIONAL CORP.
310 South Michigan Avenue
Chicago, Illinois 60604